AF375231

This book belongs to

____

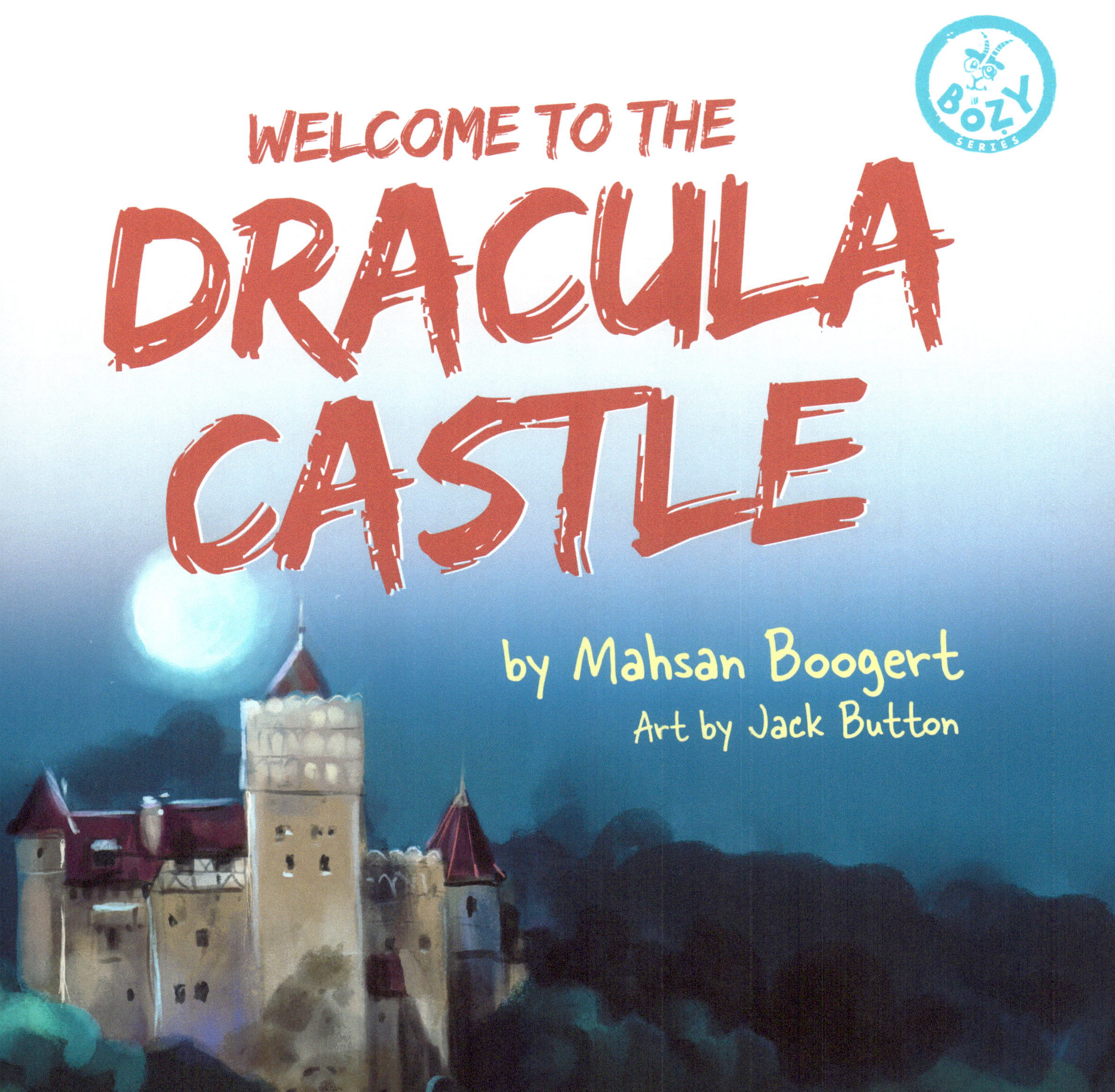

WELCOME TO THE
DRACULA
CASTLE
by Mahsan Boogert
Art by Jack Button
BOZY
SERIES

Hi friends! This is Bozy the goat!

Do you like castles?

I love castles—even the haunted ones.

Come along with me as we experience the magic
of Dracula's castle! It's in the region known as
Transylvania, in a country named Romania.

Here we are...Dracula's castle.

Join me—if you dare—as I go inside.
It's a little bit scary!

You can hold my hand if you'd like.

I'm sure you are wondering who lived in a such a mysterious castle, way high up on the top of giant hill!

Let me introduce you to
Prince Vlad the Third, the Prince of Wallachia.

He is better known as Count Dracula—the one and the only Count Dracula on earth.

I am sure you've heard his name, or read about him in books, or seen him in cartoons and movies. When Dracula's name is mentioned, all of us—even a goat like me—get scared.

I get shivers running up and down my body and tail when I think of a creature that lives for hundreds of years and drinks human blood to stay young.

Someone who vanishes when he sees the sun.

Someone with big fangs and long ears.

I think Dracula may be the scariest creature to have ever roamed the earth!

STOP! Now take a deep breath—because what
I just told you is NOT true!

The real Prince Vlad was a human—just like you.
He was not a weird creature at all.

He did not have big fangs, and he could not make
himself vanish. He was simply a normal person.

He was born in a normal family,
with a mom and a dad.

Prince Vlad ate his meals at the dining table, and actually ate yummy foods, not creepy things that scary monsters eat.

One of his favorite foods was stuffed cabbage. Do you like stuffed cabbage? I like it a lot.

He never slept in a dark coffin—like you may have seen in movies. He had a nice bed—and a warm blanket.

He was married to a real woman
and had several children.

He was kind to his friends and family.

He even liked flowers—especially roses.

Prince Vlad became the king of Romania after his father was killed by enemies. He loved his country and fought hard to keep enemies from coming to Romania.

Because of his strict, harsh behavior toward his enemies, he was given the name Dracula, a name that means *devil*.

In order to defend Romania,
Prince Vlad fought off many soldiers, mainly from
Turkey and the rest of the Ottoman Empire.

After many years of fighting for his country,
Prince Vlad was killed by his enemies.

The castle has been remodeled over the years, and more towers have been added.

Many kings and queens have lived here, but in the last 100 years, the castle has belonged to Queen Marie's family.

Queen Marie of Greater Romania was the wife of King Ferdinand.

The castle originally belonged to the people of Brasov in Romania, and since Queen Marie was so kind to them, the people gave the castle to her as a gift.

Queen Marie lived there
with her children for many years.

The huge castle now belongs
to her grandchildren.

Now you have learned a lot about the real history of Count Dracula and his castle.

It wasn't scary at all.

I think it's time for me to vanish!

See you on my next adventure...

Interesting notes to parents

From Vlad Tepes to the Myth of Count Dracula

Prince Vlad III , also known as Count Dracula, was born in 1431 in Transylvania, the second son of Vlad II Dracul who was a member of the Order of the Dragon, a chivalric order established by the Holy Roman Emperor to defend Christianity against the Ottoman Turks. After his father was killed in 1447, Vlad III and his younger brother were held captive by the Ottoman Empire. Vlad III regained his throne in 1456 with the help of the Hungarian king, and he ruled Wallachia for several years, during which time he gained a reputation for being a fierce and ruthless leader.

Image via Wikipedia.org

The name "Dracula" is derived from Vlad III's father's name, "Dracul," which means "devil" in Romanian.

Vlad III is often associated with the fictional character Count Dracula created by author Bram Stoker, although the historical figure and the literary character differ significantly. Stoker's novel drew inspiration from various sources, including the legends and folklore surrounding Vlad Tepes and his reputation as a ruthless ruler.

While Vlad is remembered as a historical figure and a national hero in Romania, his association with the fictional character of Dracula has made him a popular subject in literature, film, and popular culture.

According to history, Vlad Tepes never lived in Bran Castle, although he was imprisoned there at one point at the end of his reign. Vlad died in battle in 1476.

About the Author

Mahsan is a medical doctor, working in neuroscience research for most of her career. She is a Persian/American and has lived in the U.S. for 23 years. Following her passion for life and historical places, she has begun writing educational books for children. Mahsan's purpose in writing is to pique children's interest in learning about historical places. This inspiring travel-based series focuses on UNESCO sites and monuments all over the world. Mahsan's goal is for her books to inspire young children, offer interesting information about wonderful places, and show how people lived in the past.

More than a thousand of her Bozy books have already been donated to children's hospitals.

This Bran Fortress certificate was issued on November 19, 1377 by Louis of Anjou, the king of Poland and Hungary.

www.ingramcontent.com/pod-product-compliance
Lightning Source LLC
Chambersburg PA
CBHW042031110726
48010CB00008B/300